The
Success
State of
Mind

Don Kracke
Lee Whipple

KRACKE

DON KRACKE is the author of the Doubleday best seller HOW TO TURN YOUR IDEA INTO A MILLION DOLLARS. He co-wrote the nationally syndicated comic strip YANKEE DOODLES and with design partner Rodger Johnson created the title designs for the movie STAR TREK II. Don and Rodger are the founders of one of the United States' premiere graphic arts studios and have won over 300 awards for their creative work. In the late 60s and early 70s Don created and marketed Rickie Tickie Stickies (those little flowers that were stuck on everything, 90,000,000 sold) and since has created and brought to market over 1,200 other new products. He is a creative consultant to numerous companies, including the Coca Cola Company, The Campbell Soup Company, General Mills, Rubbermaid, Corning, and Mattel. In his spare time, Don has created one of the world's largest, most successful home fashion design and new product development companies, THE DESIGN CENTER. Products developed by "The Center" have exceeded one billion dollars in retail sales. Don has appeared on "The Oprah Winfrey Show," "Nightline," "The Merv Griffin Show," "The CBS Evening News," and numerous other television and radio programs. He is a frequent lecturer at west-coast universities, including his alma mater, U.C.L.A; his topic "Creativity in Business, Reward if Found." Don's drawings appear on almost every page of THE SUCCESS STATE OF

MIND. Along with his drawings (which he positions somewhere between The New Yorker and Mad Magazine schools
of journalistic art), Don has contributed from his business
experience approximately half of the one-liners, anecdotes,
and war stories that make up the book.

WHIPPLE

LEE WHIPPLE is the author of three books, two college texts, in the area of business and communication, and a true-life novel. His novel WHOLE AGAIN was a *Reader's Digest* book-of-the-month selection and has been translated into several foreign languages. He has contributed chapters to three other texts, edited a major section in a medical reference book, and written and produced an eight volume video series on "the high-performance team." Lee has also been published in a variety of both academic and popular periodicals, including *National Review, The Journal of Rehabilitation Medicine, Production Engineering, Home Education, Motorhome,* and *Galaxy Science Fiction Magazine.* His magazine work runs the gamut from technical articles to short stories, humorous essays, and poetry. Lee has, along with his writing career, become a highly successful business consultant. He advises in the areas of business strategy and organizational development. Clients include General Motors, Bristol-Myers Squibb, Mead Johnson, The Department of Labor, The State of Michigan, and many others. He personally advises the chief officer in several organizations and was instrumental in the formation of one of the earliest CEO networks. In the course of his consulting career Lee has on several occasions played the role of turnaround manager, assuming internal positions. In this capacity he served as the president and CEO of The Institute for the Advancement of

Prostheticsics and as general manager of the western division of The John Henry Company. He has served terms as a member of the board of directors of two corporations. Lee lectures regularly at major universities and to business groups. He has been featured on "The Today Show" on NBC and numerous other television and radio news and talk shows. His undergraduate and graduate degrees are from Michigan State University.

CONTENTS

*You may experience minor turbulence or
a change in pressure during takeoff ...*

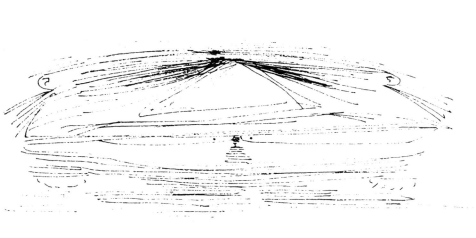

A thumbnail sketch—

Introduction

This is a book about how successful people think about themselves and things in general–*the success state of mind*–and the action that this mental state engenders. The book is in the form of quotes and one-liners, illustrated with little stories, anecdotes, drawings, and the occasional longer quotation. It is prescriptive–in all instances we take a position.

You'll find that we don't always agree with the professors or the latest fads and that we even take a certain puckish joy in spearing the pompous or ridiculous, however universally enshrined. This book is not for the faint hearted, no punches pulled.

We do not expect that you will always agree with us: we will present our case on its merits and leave the verdict to you.

Following is an overview of our book, *a thumbnail sketch—*

The Success State of Mind moves from the philosophical to the practical, general to specific. First in broad terms we discuss success, developing a personal definition and perspective. Next we explore the point of view necessary for success, the mind set that unleashes human potential and opens new worlds. The central portion of the book offers practical advice: pointing out pitfalls, bear traps to stay out of; presenting precepts, trail craft for both apprentice and journeyman. The concluding section is about leadership. Our "final word" is on personal goals.

Read the book front to back, or dive in here and there as you please–there is a subject index at the back of the book for those who like to skip around. In less than five minutes you'll have our advice on each subject covered and an example or story to drive it home.

This is not a textbook; it is a highly personal view. We make no claim to being methodical or comprehensive.

We believe that if you follow the prescriptions (and absorb the spirit) in *The Success State of Mind* you will increase your chances of gaining the winners circle, along with something far more valuable: you will enjoy getting there. And "getting there," as Robert Townsend told us in *Up the Organization* more than twenty years ago, " isn't half the fun–it's all the fun."

We would like to thank Skip Hogan, Dr. Olga Holden, Steve Reim, and Jim Shaberg for serving as reviewers and offering valuable criticism. Also, thanks to Michelle Whipple for her help in preparing the manuscript, and to Silver Spur Publishing and to our families for their support and patience.

L.W.
D.K.

"Winning isn't everything; it's the only thing!"

-John Wayne in the 1953 movie Trouble Along the Way

Success, two sides to the story

Vince Lombardi quotations make us wince, not because of the quotes themselves (we love 'um) or even because a few of the catchier lines attributed to Lombardi were actually delivered by John Wayne in a melodrama. Our discomfort stems from the one-dimensional character the quotes portray the great coach to be.

Vince Lombardi—

I firmly believe that any man's finest hour—his greatest fulfillment to all he holds dear—is that moment when he has worked his heart out in a good cause and lies exhausted on the field of battle victorious.

Wait a minute! *Finest* hour? *Greatest* fulfillment to all he holds dear? Didn't this guy have a family, friends, a spiritual life ...? Of course he did. Those who knew him well often speak about this side of the man, his love for people, his commitment to human decency and civilization, his belief in God. But it doesn't often come through in his *public* words. The more human side of Lombardi, so to speak, was private. Lombardi must be listened to with this in mind, or the message gets distorted.

Will Rogers, another often quoted American hero, strikes a note very different from Lombardi, but he presents the same sort of problem. Will Rogers, beloved humorist and homespun philosopher—

You must judge a man's greatness by how much he will be missed.... What constitutes a life well spent? Love and admiration from our fellow man is all that anyone can ask.

Hold on! Show business is not known to favor the big hearted. How did a guy like Will Rogers ever become a success in a tough town like Hollywood? Where did the grit to survive and the drive to excel come from? The answer: Will Rogers was deep down a tireless worker and a scrapper, as well as a great humanitarian. The highly motivated, tough side of Will Rogers was never publicized. It wasn't part of his *public* image. So we must listen to him with that in mind, or once again the message gets distorted.

Balance is required in both instances, Lombardi and Will Rogers. Listening exclusively to the Lombardi or the Will Rogers public voice, or others in similar veins, can lead to lopsided lives: providing an excuse on the one hand for obsessive drives, on the other for timidity. Balance! A man or woman does not have to choose between being an iron bar or a bowl of mush.

Let's look at another American hero, a recent one, Lee Iacocca, where we have the advantage of being able to see more than one side. Lee Iacocca, president and spark plug of Chrysler Corporation in its most difficult and glorious hour, listen—

Whatever you do in life—sell advertising, make bread, build cars, you name it—you've got to want to be the best ... if a person is going to do a good job, he's got to like coming to work. He's got to say to himself: 'I'm going to help produce something great today,' and he's got to say that every day....

Iacocca, listen again—

You know, of all the tough jobs I've had in my life, none has been tougher or more important to me than my job as a dad.... People used to ask me: 'How could somebody as busy as you go to all those swim meets and recitals?': I just put them down on my calendar.... I pray for good health for my kids, my family, my friends.... I never pray to my God that Chrysler can make $20 a share ... or anything as unimportant as that.

Success, two sides to the story.

Balance, the secret of success.

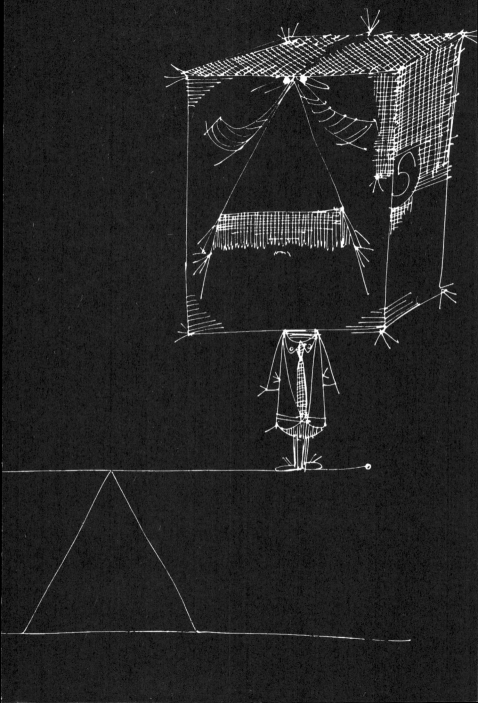

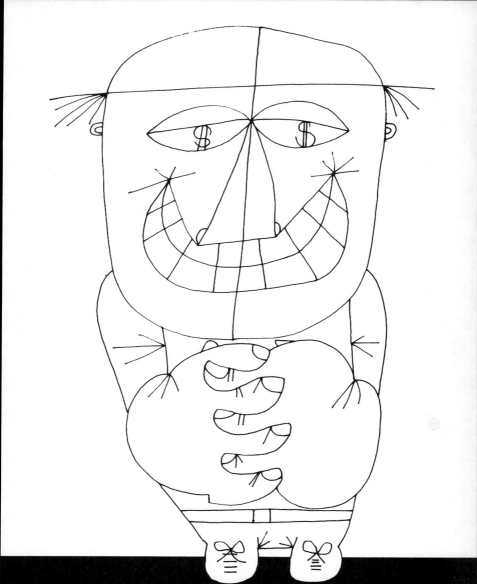

> *"[T]he squalid cash interpretation*
> *put on the word success is our national disease."*

-William James from a letter to H.G. Wells

Money is *not* success

Money is a good way of keeping score, no doubt about it. But it's not the only way. It's only one way and not even the best way or the most important—

There's a guy in a Madame d' Aulnoy fairy tale who wears golden boots. He's a foppish loser who in the end gets pushed over a cliff into the sea by a princess who made the mistake of marrying him. He paid a high price to make a big splash. You sink very quickly when you're wearing golden boots. This guy was *not* successful, even though he was extremely rich.

Now don't get us wrong. Neither of us believes that money is evil. We like the stuff. It allows you to travel to interesting places in comfort, tasting new things along the way; but that's minor. The important thing that money does is allow you the freedom to choose your work and then do it the very best that you can. Money can be a good thing. It can be loads of fun and even assist you in pursuit of success, but that's the extent of it. Money and success are *not* the same thing.

Having the love and respect of those around you, having your spiritual life in order, and doing whatever it is you do on this earth just as well as you can: now that's success. All three elements, every one of them, creatively balanced, are in our view essential to success. And in the end, you can't buy any of them.

"Jimmy's an excellent convict. He's a lousy citizen."

-Rev. Rex Burns
speaking of Jimmy Lee Smith, the "Onion Field" Killer

The relativity of success

Rev. Burns, longtime counselor of Jimmy Lee Smith, made the above comment upon one of Jimmy's many returns to Prison—

Jimmy Lee Smith is a lousy citizen if ever there was one. He has been arrested five times and has spent less than one year of his adult life out of custody. Even so, as was told in Joseph Wambaugh's novel *The Onion Field*, he is an excellent convict: so he keeps getting paroled. Smith is typical of the sixty percent of paroled felons who return to prison within two years. Rev. Burns captured wonderfully the folly of the parole process–the assumption that success as a convict predicts success as a citizen–in his comment. All prison psychologists and parole board members should have Rev. Burn's words framed on their walls.

So should the rest of us.

We all, one way or another, make the same general error: success here means success there, when it ain't necessarily so. Dr. Peter isolated a widespread instance of this in his famous *Peter Principle* : people get promoted based on irrelevant skill and performance to jobs they can't do–their "level of incompetence"–and remain unproductively there for the rest of their careers. Everyone knows this, yet people are promoted every day based solely on success at things totally irrelevant to their new positions.

Success *here* doesn't always mean success *there*; it may have nothing to do with it whatever. A little thought shows this to be true, but it's so easy to miss a trick.

We have a good friend who found himself in a harbor in the Bahamas without a captain for his ninety-foot yacht. A guy rowed out to the yacht to apply, around dinner time. Captain Bob, let's call him. He brought his wife. Captian Bob borrowed a diving mask and a spear-gun and dove into the water. Back, soon, he came with a beautiful grouper. Captain Bob's wife went down to the galley and, presto, produced a meal that would shame the Sign of the Dove. Wow! Our friend hired Captain Bob on the spot.

The next day, hopelessly lost, Captain Bob wrecked the boat on a reef. True story.

Captain Bob was a good fisherman, his wife a fine cook, but that did not make him a navigator. Jimmy Lee Smith is an outstanding convict; he knows how to play that game. But as a citizen, Jimmy turns up a loser every time. The mistake is so easy to make: success *here* means success *there* but it ain't necessarily so.

Success is relative.

The mighty engine of success

Scholar and author Joseph Campbell attributed his notable success–great popular appeal, while maintaining the respect of the academic community–to following his bliss. It delayed financial achievement and comfortable living, but the ultimate result was a life he treasured and would trade for none other—

As a boy Joseph Campbell fell in love with mythology, the masks of the northwestern American Indians in particular in the American Museum of Natural History in New York City. He deepened and expanded this love throughout the remainder of his life, writing classic texts, comprising the entire mythological history of mankind, as well as popular works. He did a television series with Bill Moyers, served as a story consultant to Stephen Spielberg in making the motion picture *Star Wars*....

"I was held to the *life* of my subject," Campbell said, "and this is the thing that built whatever it is I have had as a career...."

Campbell's varied achievements and awards could fill a book. You don't choose success like that: it chooses you, you're *driven*.

That's right, *driven*. Oh we know, that's a dirty word these days. It's supposed to be some sort of disease. Don't you believe it. Psychologists be hanged: anyone who ends up really good at anything—choose your hero, Leonardo da Vinci to Henry Ford—and enjoys any measure of success is driven by a powerful internal, sometimes irrational, desire to do or learn or be something. "I did just what I wanted to do," said Campbell. "It took a little courage at first ... who wants you to do just what you want to do; they've all got plans for you. But you can make it happen...." Identifying your bliss, daring to be *driven* in hot pursuit, that's the first bold step towards success.

Drive: an internal desire born of dreams. It renews itself, day after day. You want to! Not because of what you'll get, that's *pull*. Not because there's a gun at your head, that's *push*. Want-to is *drive*. It's the only motivator that lasts, the only one that will get you to the finish line. Frederick Herzberg established this in benchmark research years ago. Money and status, and other external reasons for doing things, can fire a guy up if his bank account is low or he can't get any respect.... But get very much money or status and more is like putting water in the tank–it won't ignite. The only thing you can't get enough of, that burns forever, is bliss.

So pick something you love to be your life's work, and don't let anybody make you feel guilty by sticking a "workaholic" label on you if you'd rather work than play golf on Saturday. Recreation, family commitments, sure. Balance, yes! But don't get that confused with a lack of passion for the work that you do. Being crazy about your work is a gift, not a curse. It's an essential element, one of the secrets–the *mighty engine*–of success.

Follow your bliss.

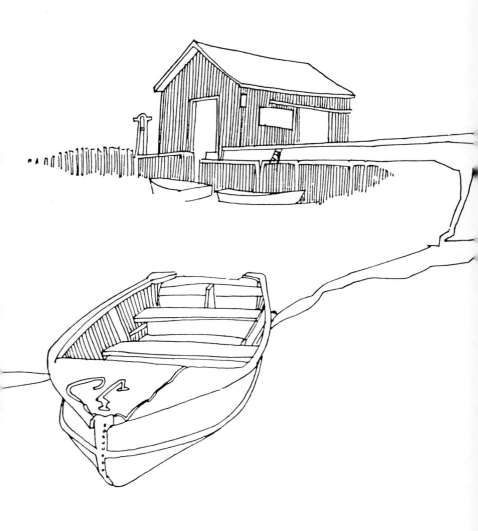

A responsible drawing ...

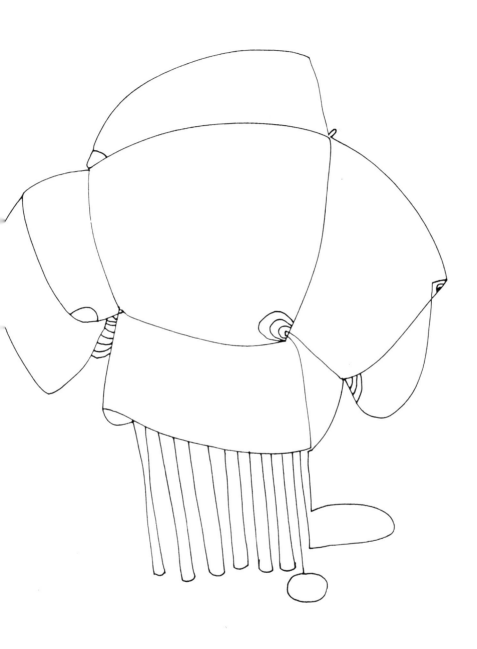

An irresponsible drawing ...

"Fairy tales can come true. It can happen to you,
If you're young at heart... [and have nerves of steel]."

-an old song

Success story

A few years back *Esquire* magazine ran a piece on *the big score*. Odds were given–how arrived at, God knows–for the chances of writing a bestselling novel, turning a start-up venture in short order into a megabucks success, and so forth. The odds were a thousand, or so, to one most of the time as we recall. About right, it seems, maybe optimistic. But it happens, and that's important: "Fairy tales can come true [sing along]. It can happen to you, if you're young at heart...."

Let us tell you the story of Bob Tezak of Joliet, Illinois—

Bob, as a young man, tried this and that without much success. This didn't surprise anybody. He had *not* been voted most likely to succeed in high school. Nobody expected him to end up in prison, but that's about as far out on a limb as anyone would go. Bob thought he was special, however, and that he was going to make it big, somehow.

On a visit to Kentucky, Bob met a man who had invented a card game. The fellow was an official in the international Kiwanis Club who traveled a lot. Over the years the fellow had sold a number of sets of his game to people he had met and worked with, each set handmade. People liked it. They wrote and ordered more cards (the game was murder on on the cards) when the first set wore out. The Kiwanis fellow had built up a small business. Sales of about five thousand dollars a year, growing a little, maybe.

Bob loved the game, to play, and saw it at the same time as serious business. He thought the world would love the game too, that people would go nuts over it, and that he could get rich in the process. He was sure of it! He was, as his friends and family told him, crazy. By all odds, this was true.

The international Kiwanis fellow wanted eighty thousand dollars for the game. Ridiculous! Twenty years at current sales to return the investment. No marketing or distribution in place. No mass production. No prospects, no plan....

Money was tight, interest rates high. Bob had some savings, not enough, and no experience in the game business. All the business people Bob talked to about his desire to turn this little game into a fortune laughed. If you know anything about the game business, you know why. Bob's dream was from an investment-banking point of view the equivalent of selling snowballs to Eskimos: they don't really need them, they already have them, and the market has been cornered by God. The game business is like that, especially the part about God.

Bob went ahead. He borrowed the money needed to go with his savings and bought the game. No one could be that dumb!

Long story short: the game companies laughed at him

when he approached them with a spiffed-up version of the game. Investors were not interested in backing him to market the game himself. Dead end.

So, door-to-door, he placed the game in some Chicago-area stores. He hand assembled the decks in a little building behind his father's flower shop, answering the phone for an occasional reorder while he worked. He would pretend to put people on hold every once in a while as a joke.

More door to door, more hand assembly, and all of a sudden nothing happened. But Bob kept at it and pretty soon he was making a living. Then, to everyone's surprise, a pretty good living. And in a few years—after continued hard work and gutsy expansions and going deeper in debt and almost losing everything several times—to everyone's absolute astonishment, he became, just like in the movies, a jillionaire. Yup. Factories all over the world, his own jet, his little card game outselling *Monopoly*, establishing itself as the number one selling game in the world.

Uno.

"Fairy tales can come true. It can happen to you, if you're young at heart ... [and have nerves of steel]."

*Man eating
tiger...*

-a fact

Success pills and potions

Too often people seek something that they can buy, or a magic rite that they can perform, that will result in surefire success. There's no shortage of products and proffers—

Attend this seminar, or that, with the latest guru of motivational psychology or real-estate or stock-market voodoo and, presto, the world will be yours....

Acquire this or that degree, from this or that school, and it's home free!

Gain five years experience with XYZ company and you can write your own ticket....

Become a friend of so-and-so and you've got the inside track....

And, yes, read this book or another and you will learn everything you need to know and it will magically bring success....

No way!

No single thing—no course, no degree, not this book, not any other—creates success. No collection of *things* creates success. No one else can do it for you. Knowledge is helpful, insight essential, contacts can be important; but in the end it's performance, what you produce, that counts.

It's *always* up to you.

There is no success pill!

You've got to want to yourself, be ready, willing and able—and it's a little different every time.

The first person you've got to convince is yourself!

-*anonymous*

The success state of mind

Eric Berne, the psychologist, suggests that we all have "life scripts"–story lines, programmed in childhood–that we act out over and over in different ways throughout our lives.

Life scripts explain why one person consistently turns adversity into success, while another turns golden opportunities into failure. Eric Berne's notion, with room for exceptions, gross misfortune or the odd run of luck, rings true. We collect in our heads a book of stories, sometimes about ourselves, sometimes about others, some truth, some myth, that we come to live by. We tell ourselves these stories over and over and, lo and behold, for better or worse, they come true. We seek out and conform to, or if need be create, the reality that confirms our beliefs. The *pygmalion effect*: perceived possibility becomes probability and then reality. The stories we tell ourselves have points, and we *get* them....

So why not choose our stories more purposely and purposefully: to inspire and energize, never to discourage or provide an excuse when we stumble and fall. Who needs another woebegone tale to trip us up or drag us down.

Why not tell yourself stories that *work*?

As a young man, one of the authors of this book attended a talk by a poetess in her sixties who had recently enjoyed the publication of her first collection of poems. She had been writing poetry since she was six. The audience was college age, mostly would-be writers: a discouraged lot for the most part, many of them half way to giving up before they had really begun. The poetess listened patiently in the question-and-answer session that followed her talk as one young person after another told of their difficulties in becoming published and asked her advice on breaking into print. Many told a discouraging story to illustrate how unfair and impossible it was.

Unpublished writers have a habit of collecting stories, you see, about the publishing industry, horror stories, mostly true. There's the one, for instance, about the guy who took a prize-winning, internationally acclaimed novel and had it retyped with a new title and a made-up author's name. He submitted it to twenty-five major publishing houses. It was turned down cold by every one, not even an encouraging word. Dozens of similar stories make the rounds.

Trying to become a writer can be discouraging business. It's true. The poetess knew this, but she also knew that being discouraged gets you nowhere: she had somehow found a way to keep her spirits up and the creativity flowing through many years of rejection. She listened patiently to the stories of editorial favoritism, shortsightedness, and outright stupidity, attempting to give practical advice, and then something snapped. The poetess faced her audience of gloomy would-be writers and gave them a good scolding and a pep

talk all rolled into one, an inspired and inspiring speech—
   "Tell yourself different stories," she said. "Put all this gloom in a Gothic novel, if you must be gloomy. Sell it to your readers, not yourselves! Tell yourselves stories of heroism and hope....
   "Try telling yourself this story," she said, "and then talk to me about impossible:
   "Aleksandr Solzhenitsyn was in the labor camps of the Soviet Union, deprived of the basic tools and the time to write. So he wrote in his head, while he labored, memorizing each line. One week each month he recited the entire text of the work in progress, fixing it in his mind.
   "Books later, being diagnosed as having terminal cancer, he was sent from the camps into domestic exile; one of those sterile prison towns in the middle of icy nowhere, but paradise by comparison to the camps. He now had the time and the basic tools to write. Yet his illness was terminal. He had only, they told him, six months, a year at best, to live. He feverishly pushed ahead with his writing.
   "A new problem confronted him," she continued, "the secret police. Dissidents' homes were searched regularly. Solzhenitsyn kept his writing in 'hidey holes' about the town, retrieving only a few pages–a volume of paper that could be destroyed in seconds if state officials knocked at his door– to work on at any one time. He pushed on. He miraculously recovered from cancer and wrote in exile for twelve years, with no conceivable possibility of publishing his work. But

the opportunity came—

"Solzhenitsyn made acquaintances who offered to help smuggle his writing to the West. He took the chance–those helping him might prove to be agents of the Soviet state. He transferred his work to microfilm, a tedious process using a single electric bulb. The risk was immense, greater than any he had taken thus far....

"You know the rest of the story," she said, smiling warmly at her audience. "Solzhenitsyn's books now appear in nearly every library and book store in the free world. He followed his books to the West and writes here a free man today.

"Choose your story!" she exhorted her audience. "Tell yourself the awful truth about the publishing industry, or tell yourself about Aleksandr Solzhenitsyn....

"Failure to place your work," she concluded, "is nothing but an argument with the world about your capabilities as a writer and the worth of what you have to say; and stories, your business, are always, one way or another, arguments, attempts to persuade. Thomas Babington Macaulay said it, 'Narration is the mighty engine of argument.'

"You're writers, for Heaven's sake! Argue, persuade! Use stories to your benefit, not your detriment. Tell what stories you will to the world, but tell yourself stories that argue for success."

At least one person in her audience, a young man named Lee Whipple, was listening.

You're reading one of his several books.

Sow a thought,
  and you reap an act;
Sow an act,
  and you reap a habit;
Sow a habit,
  and you reap a character;
Sow a character,
  and you reap a destiny.

-Anonymous
Quoted by Samuel Smiles,
Life and Labor [1887]

-John Dryden

The security of mediocrity

A major company wanted a *bold and creative* new approach to selling its products. "Oh boy," thought the young advertising guy assigned to the account, and away he went putting together just what they had asked for. Verve, color, zest....

Next scene: The young advertising guy presents the campaign to a vice president in the client company. The VP smiles uncomfortably. "Look," he says, "this is very nice stuff, but I think the culture here is a little too conservative for this. Maybe we should look at something a bit more conventional...."

No sale.

That's the way it is, over and over, in one company, government agency, and university after another. It's avoiding a mistake, not doing something right, that counts. "Don't make waves. Don't back no losers," as Milton Rakove put it in his book about Chicago's political machine–and that, sadly, is precisely what many large organizations are, political machines. Just do what you're told, don't make waves, and you'll do *OK*. You'll get a promotion when it comes your turn, get your twenty year pin, and collect a gold watch in the end. But what about all those years of mediocrity and meaningless labor?

What profits a man who gains a corner office but loses

his soul? Besides that, and to the point of this book, it's no way to succeed. We mean *succeed!* not just do OK. To do one's best, achieve any measure of excellence, a man or woman must allow the pendulum to swing. You have to push the limits. There's a time to play safe, and a time *not* to!

Check out the careers of really successful people. Pick any one you like. You'll find setbacks, failures. Many have been fired once or twice; some have gone broke. Benjamin Franklin, Abraham Lincoln, the Wright brothers, Thomas Edison, Vince Lombardi, Henry Ford to Lee Iacocca....

It's your batting average, not the game-score or the number of foul balls, that counts.

Who cares who's ahead at the beginning or in the middle of the race?

You've got to *play*, not play it safe. If you're *not* missing the basket now and then, you're not putting the ball up enough....

So go ahead, take a shot! Get in the game. Risk failure. Or settle one way or another–no matter what the title or how much the job pays–for being the water boy.

"It is only by risking our persons from one hour to another that we live at all. And often enough our faith beforehand in an uncertain result is the only thing that makes the result come true."

—*William James*

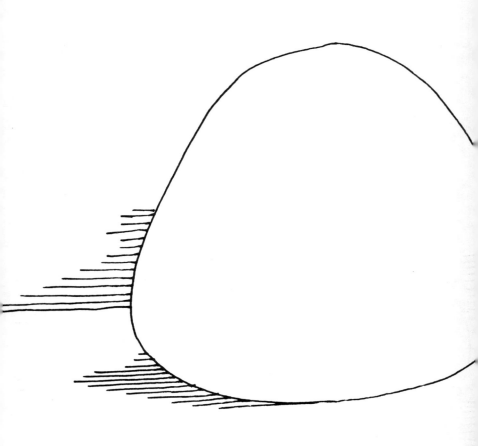

"Nuthin'. What's new with you?"

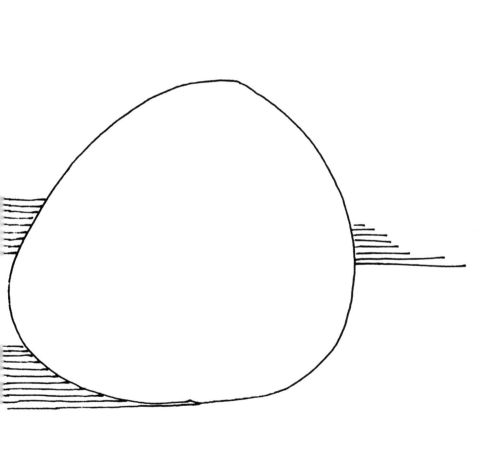

Unless you're doing something that might get you fired, you're probably not doing much of anything.

-*anonymous*

There is no *They*

How many times have you heard the question: "What do *They* want? *What do They want me to do?*" The organization, the committee, the client group, the voters, the bosses ...

"*What do They want me to do?*"

In the long run, it really doesn't matter.

Now that's a shocking attitude, we know. Sounds cavalier, rash. But it's the right answer. The one that will ultimately result in points on the score board, satisfied customers, profitable organizations ... and personal success.

"Who cares what *They* want?" as we've heard a friend of ours, one of the top creative people in the advertising industry, say to a young artist worrying over what some important client wants him or her to create. "Forget 'um, do it right!"

Our friend's injunction usually scares the daylights out of the young person: "F-F-F-Forget'um,"he or she stammers.

"You got it," says our friend, shifting into his kindly uncle routine, hand on the young person's shoulder. "If you know what it is you're trying to do–if you've defined the problem correctly, know the goal–go ahead. Pursue it, do it. Do it right! You're the one you need to please. The right answer, not the one *They* think is right, is the only answer you want.

"There is no *They!*"

The basis for our friend's advice is simple:

If you're doing a job you know how to do (unless you're a trainee, why else would someone be paying you to do it?) you're the one who is closest to the work, best informed, and knows best how to go about it. Ask lots of questions, get advice if needed. Make sure you're on target as to the final outcome, the *end result* that must be produced. After that, make it happen. Period. Everyone will be happy in the long run.

Giving someone something they want that doesn't work never gets anyone very far: being kept around as a reward for being compliant is the best you'll ever do. Yuk!

Long-run success comes from creating the right answer, even if it's unpopular at first. This takes guts, it's true. Every once in a while somebody gets fired for having the self confidence and conviction to do his job the best that he can. That's rare—and no place to hang around anyway. No future. If you know what you're doing, do it and let the chips fall. Trusting your own experience, expertise, and instinct is not a sure bet but it sure is the best bet, and the only one that pays off in the end.

"I was only following orders."

-the authors

We all need heroes

The Armadillo: he has a hide one-quarter inch of armor plate thick and can hold his breath for over six minutes; he can jump four times his own height straight up in the air; he eats fire ants and scorpions for lunch....

'Tis true, he doesn't have the flowing lines of the gazelle or the bright colors of the parrot. But then he's not the sort who ever wanted to be an assistant-assistant vice president anyway.

"By heaven, kings could learn something about nobility from these roughnecks of mine."

-George Rogers Clark
from the historical novel Long Knife
by James Alexander Thom

Heroes and more heroes

Colonel George Rogers Clark (elder brother of William, of "Lewis and Clark") led about one hundred men on a winter march from Kaskaskia in the southern part of the old Northwest Territory to take Fort Sackville at Vincennes. The march covered over a hundred miles across three different flood plains during a winter thaw, water chest deep much of the way—

It was a desperate situation: General (Lord Hennery) Hamilton, famed for his practice of buying American scalps from Indians, had pushed his way south from Detroit and threatened to establish his brutal dominance on the western frontier and possibly extend it south into Kentucky. Colonel Clark, greatly outnumbered, assessed that surprise and fighting spirit were his only assets. He decided to press them to the limit, undertaking what was by any reasonable judgement an impossible mission: a surprise attack on Hamilton in his strongest position, Fort Sackville.

During the early part of the march to Fort Sackville, Clark gave the task of securing game and preparing the evening meal to a different company within his troops each day.

This turned quickly into a competition among the men, each company trying to outdo the feasts already presented. The result was the consumption of huge quantities of meat, a defense against the next day's exhaustion and cold. The feasts, accompanied by bonfires, contests, and singing, fed the troops in spirit as well as body. Colonel Clark feasted and reveled with his men, more than once breaking out rations of rum to toast their courage and spirit.

During the first several days, Clark worked his way constantly from the front to the back of his troops, then up and back again, physically touching his soldiers, smiling and joking about the brutal conditions, voicing his admiration for them one-and-all. One soldier wrote in his journal that Clark must have marched three miles for every one marched by the soldiers he led.

The water grew deeper and the cold more bitter, as the trek progressed. Trees were felled and dugout canoes fashioned to carry weapons and the few remaining provisions. Game grew scarce, then nonexistent.

Days passed with no high ground to camp on, no fires at night to warm body or spirit, and no food. Clark praised his troops endlessly, swearing no other soldiers in history possessed the stamina or spirit of those around him now—and he kept their purpose, to stop "Lord Hennery the scalp merchant," before them always. "We'll get him soon, boys," he assured them. "We'll put an end to his unholy reign...."

A small island was finally reached a dozen miles from Fort Sackville. A passing canoe containing enough meat to make a thin broth for the troops was commandeered. Small fires were risked to cook the broth and warm the troops.

They were within striking distance now but the water was too deep to go further. Time and again the scouts returned, reporting the way impassable in yet another direction. The only way open was back. Clark, in a moment of dejection, let slip the confident demeanor that he had displayed from the start. He stood with stooped shoulders and bowed head at the edge of the little island receiving a report from recently returned scouts. It was nearly dark, the icy evening chill setting in harder than on any night of the march. Too late, Clark realized his error. Behind him, the watching troops were near panic, ready to turn back in mutiny.

Clark dipped his hand in the water, poured a little powder from his horn into it, and began to blacken his face, as would be done for a night raid. A look from him had his captains doing the same. Then, letting out a war whoop, he waded into the icy waters, waist, then chest deep. The troops followed.

All night he felt his way, step at a time, zigzagging a treacherous course through the water. He sent his scouts ahead with orders to call back constantly that there was shallow water ahead, and toward morning they miraculously found it and a path to Vincennes....

Fort Sackville was taken, as Colonel Clark had planned, by surprise, and the fearless fighting spirit of he and his men!

"The greatest obstacle to being heroic is the doubt whether one may not be going to prove one's self a fool; the truest heroism is to resist the doubt; and the profoundest wisdom is to know when it ought to be resisted, and when to be obeyed."

-Nathaniel Hawthorne

A caution

A number of years back, business dictated that an investment-banker friend of ours live in Florida for a while. He found himself looking around for a place to settle in. His permanent home is on a lake in upstate New York. He likes lakes, his family likes lakes. So he began looking at places close to the water.

Being a northerner our friend has a visceral fear of alligators. They scare the daylights out of him! Statistically, the chances of being eaten by an alligator are infinitesimal. He knows. Actuarially, it's a safe bet. OK. But the way he sees it you only have to get eaten by an alligator once to have it spoil your whole day.

"Paranoia is a survival trait," as he is fond of saying.

So he went ahead and asked those dumb (go ahead and call him a "Snowbird") Yankee questions.

Here's how the conversation went, again and again and again—

"Any alligators in this lake?"

"No, no..."

"Safe to swim here?"

"Sure."

"You swim here?"

"No."

This oft repeated conversation with Floridians now comes to our friend's mind whenever he's thinking of taking a swim of any kind. Investment, product development, expansion, acquisition... He asks the same "dumb" questions.

"Any alligators in this lake...?"

Our friend is eminently successful. He remains unabashedly paranoid and wary of advice from nonswimmers.

BOLDNESS *Caution*

BALANCE

Assumptions

Assumptions have received more cheap shots than Cleveland—

Chumptions, they're called. Or *dumbtions*. The mnemonic of *ass u & me* as the component parts of the word *assume* (assume makes an ass of u & me) crosses the blackboards of beginning classes in business everywhere. *Don't assume nuthin'!*: the sentiment is basically sound, but the humor is low and the logic faulty.

You *can't* stop making assumptions. Operating assumptions are necessary to operate. *Ipso facto.* No way around it. You can't proceed from unknown to known, from start to finish of any solution or task, without making assumptions. They're a necessary element of productive thought and action. You can't *not* make assumptions.

What you can do is make the minimum number, make them conservatively, and test them constantly. When a businessman stops shopping and places an order for needed supplies with a vendor, he's assuming capability on the vendor's part to produce and deliver. This, at some point, if he's to do business, he must do. Even with careful investigation, even with vendor certification, there are multiple assumptions involved, right down to human nature and the weather. Bad guesses (or bad luck, reasonable assumptions that go sour) about people, the weather, or a thousand other imponderables, can sink the soundest ship. As Robert Burns told us, "The best laid schemes o' mice and men [g]ang aft a-gley." And best we not forget it!

You *must* make operating assumptions–and always you might be wrong– but you need not become comatose at this juncture. You can check and test. Check and double check, test and retest.... And you can go a step further, by *adding* assumptions, negative ones, to the others you've made: *It will be wrong! It will be late! It will be over budget! It will be ...*

Forget the happy myth of banning assumptions. Make them prudently and pessimistically instead.

Now you might be thinking this is *too* pessimistic. No, no. It's *realistic* pessimistic, and it has a happy ending. Making careful assumptions–instead of kidding yourself that you're not making any–and adding an expectation of the worst prompts you to anticipate obstacles and take measures in advance to remove them. As Murphy posits, "What can go wrong will go wrong." Face it, expect it, correct it. This isn't gloom and doom. It's good sense.

Always balance your belief in yourself and your expectation of ultimate success with conservative assumptions and an unshakable faith that things will go wrong all along the way. You'll be happy in the end, when it counts, when in spite of fortune's slings and arrows you *succeed!*

"Murphy was an optimist."

If it's more than a two-dollar bet bet on experience

Two kinds of reasoning: *apriori* and *aposteriori*. Two tools, quite different, each suited to a different job. But for all *practical* purposes one is better than the other—

First, the other, *apriori* reasoning:

Apriori reasoning is deductive, pure logic. You figure from what you know to what might be. You draw logical conclusions in chronological order, developing a hypothesis or theory. General Custer had a theory that day back in 1876 at the Little Bighorn about how he and his two hundred men would defeat a bunch of Sioux. It turned out to be a tough lesson in when and when-not to indulge in apriori thought.

Apriori thinking can go sour any number of ways: if one of the things you *know* from which you deduce your plan of action turns out not to be so, or combines with another *known* in not quite the way you had in mind, or A doesn't, after all, lead to B, or X,Y, and Z come along unexpectedly for the ride–a lot more Indians, and smarter, than you had planned on for instance–you're dead!

Remember General Custer.

Aposteriori is the alternative:

Aposteriori is inductive reasoning, based on experience not speculation. General Custer might have consulted an old Indian fighter–old Indian fighters have been around, seen a few things, *lived* through battles–and mixed his West Point theory with a little old-west savvy, then stirred the whole thing with a stick of sagebrush and spit in it for luck. That's what Old Hickory–who got to be an *old* Indian fighter–would have done we'll bet.

But General Custer had his plan, a masterpiece, no doubt, of logical steps in sequence, perfectly timed. General Custer was pure West Point, an apriori guy: he died young. It doesn't always turn out that way, of course. There's an exception to every rule.

A friend of ours at the track for instance—

He was having lunch with his wife and children at Churchhill Downs in the Eclipse restaurant overlooking the track. His nine-year-old daughter, her first time at the races, was studying the racing form. "Find a horse you like?" our friend asked, chuckling an indulgent, fatherly chuckle.

"Yup," she said, ignoring his patronizing tone, "Little Bob in the seventh." This was not the response our friend had expected. The speed and certainty of her reply was disconcerting. He might have known he was in the presence of nascent apriori reasoning. Pure logic is often lightning fast and chock-full of surprises.

"I suppose you'd like to place a bet," he teased his daughter.

"Yes," his daughter answered, "I'll bet a dollar on Little Bob."

"Minimum bet's two," he told her.

"OK," she said, after no more than a moment or two's hesitation.

Pure logic is bold....

Our friend had picked up the racing form while his daughter was considering: "Little Bob's thirty-to-one!" he exclaimed. "I thought you were supposed to be a bright kid?"

"I've made up my mind," his daughter said, reaching for her little purse.

Pure logic cares not for the odds....

"That's OK, I know you're good for it," he said, looking around, motioning for her to put her purse away. "But look, this is family: what's your system?" Apriori reasoning in the racing world is often referred to as a *system*.

"It's simple," the little girl said. "Look at the paper: Little Bob has 'No Rider.' He will have less weight to carry. And he must be a very smart horse to run races all by himself."

Our friend went to the window and placed the two-dollar bet–what else could he do?–anticipating a little lesson in the pitfalls of apriori reasoning for his daughter: "No Rider," of course, means *to be determined* and the nag would run dead last. But on this day–despite the odds and the jockey, to the little girl's surprise, astride–Little Bob won running away. Thirty to one! True story. Still, in practical matters we argue–rule superseding exception–against dependence on apriori reasoning.

Apriori thought is useful, even necessary for progress (breaking new ground) to be made. But don't rely on it exclusively unless you're operating in a vacuum, and that means you're in a laboratory not for-Goodness sake on a battle field or in the free market. Keep it down-to-earth, your aposteriori, as it were, when live ammunition is flying and you may just live (remember General Custer) to fight another day.

If it's more than a two-dollar bet, bet on experience.

"YOUTH IS WHOLLY EXPERIMENTAL."

–Robert Louis Stevenson

A decision making maxim

Because it is *not* axiomatic that green things with webbed feet, hopping about and croaking, are frogs (we all remember the fairy tale about the frog who was really a prince) most of us spend a lot of time shmozzing with green things. All of us want to (like the princess in the story, the one who kissed the frog) see deeply into things, not be fooled by surface reality.

True, appearance and reality can be tricky business. How can anyone *really* tell who's who or what's what? Nobody wants to be the guy who fired Iacocca or turned down *Rocky*. We all want to be perceptive, intuitive–every frog, after all, *might* be a prince–the kind of guy who divines truth and beauty where others see only prosaic facades and reflections of their own inadequacies. None of us wants to be that dumb guy who passed up the deal of a lifetime, said no to a prince.

"Beauty is only skin deep...."
"Don't judge a book by its cover...."
'The best things come in the smallest packages...."
"Don't throw the baby out with the bath water...."
And on and on.

OK. We know. It's true. A guy can get fooled. It can

happen to anyone!

So what happens?

Most of us bend over backwards, an inherently unbalanced posture, trying to keep from being taken in by the obvious, and we fall on our backsides. We find a smoking gun in the butler's hand and assume he's innocent *because* he's the butler. *The butler did it* is too simple. We're not one of those guys who gets fooled by the surface appearance. We're like Sherlock Holmes.

We're so smart we outsmart ourselves—

How many frogs have you gotten involved with because you secretly believed they might be princes? How many times were they?

How many new frog-products have you bought focusing totally on the upside, turning a blind eye to the negatives? Ever done that?

Ever invested in a frog-stock, accentuating the positive, ignoring the fact that the company you bought into had webbed feet and went "Ri-bit?"

Haunting sound, isn't it? "Ri-bit, Ri-bit ..."

Don't bend over backwards too far.

If it looks like a frog and croaks like a frog, if it hops around like a frog–it's probably a frog.

"Common sense is not so common."

–Voltaire

Security

Security, be it "lifetime" employment, golden parachute or government job, is only as good as the promise of payment involved: the intentions and ability of the promisor to deliver. The road to hell is paved with good intentions, and the Titanic lies on the bottom of the sea. Forget security. In the final analysis, fortune can sink you or anyone else.

Diversity will make you *more* secure. Being quick on your feet and resilient will make you even *more so*. But that's as far as it goes, as good as it gets. Sooner or later, there are only the quick and the dead.

So keep your powder dry, and don't take any wooden nickels. Trust God, but never your employer, banker, or broker....

MADE IN JAPAN

Opportunity

The Swiss used to *own* the watch business, nearly eighty percent of the sales worldwide. Thousands of Swiss citizens worked in the industry. It was a matter of national economic importance and pride—

Swiss engineers, inside the watch business, developed the quartz-crystal time keeping technology and showed it to their management. "It's not a watch," management replied. No springs, no gears.... The new technology was offensive to the old guard who had built the watch business and made it tick.

The Swiss engineers exhibited the quartz-crystal innovation at a trade show as a novelty. They didn't even bother to patent their work. Why would they? The smart guys they worked for had emphatically judged the quartz-crystal technology to have no commercial value. The Japanese attended the trade show. They found the quartz-crystal technology interesting, exciting. The rest is history. Japan now *owns* the watch business. Thousands of Japanese work in the industry. It is now *for them* a matter of national economic importance and pride....

In life opportunity knocks twice: it taps you gently on the shoulder, and then (if you don't look sharp) it may knock you in the head.

"Overnight success takes years."

from How To Turn Your Idea Into A Million Dollars

Success is a marathon

Most people don't want to hear that success is going to take a lot of time and be a lot of trouble and maybe never happen. Surefire, overnight success is more appealing, and makes a better story. Most people want to believe that Marilyn Monroe was discovered in a drug store sipping a soda and presto became a star. Or that Donald Trump entered the real-estate business one day on a whim and got a few breaks and faster than you could say "let's make a deal" he owned half of New York City....

Meteoric rises are the norm, in movies and on television. The popular press follows suit, reinforcing the myth. Right place, right time, bingo! You're swingin' from a star. Sorry but it's not like that, not even close.

The unfortunate thing about the overnight-success myth is that people who believe it go into business or head for Hollywood, or whatever, running blind, sprinting for the finish line. That's no way to run a marathon through a mine field—and that's the reality. Better to begin the race in shape, physically and mentally prepared for a long haul because that is what it's likely to be. Following is a *true* "overnight" success story, straight from the racehorses mouth—

-1967-

March. Don Kracke and his wife are driving down a California freeway. They note that a number of cars going by (this was when the *hippie* movement was in flower) are hand painted with brightly colored designs. Idea! Stick-on vinyl flowers to decorate cars, maybe trash cans, mailboxes, maybe even bathtubs and showers...? Who knows? Who would have guessed?

April. Prototype produced, company formed, trademark applied for.

May. Pepsi Cola expresses interest in using the product as a premium in a major promotion. Euphoria! Dancing in the street.

July. Deal with Pepsi falls through. First run of three thousand stick-on vinyl flowers produced. Calls made on major department stores, a few orders taken.

August. Display box designed and ordered. Sales slow, but increasing. Production expenses mount. Savings depleted.

September. Product is named "Rickie Tickie Stickies." New packaging. More expenses. Sales slow, but increasing.

November. Sales reach $8,000.

December. Sales reach $30,000. Recount: $30,000! Euphoria! Exhaustion!

-1968-

January. Sales climb. Production expenses outrun cash

flow from sales. Kids education fund tapped: something that would *never-ever*, not in a million years, be done!

February. Chicago Printed String Company, a giant, wants to buy Rickie Tickie Stickies. Euphoria! Days before the deal is to be signed, CPSC is purchased by Paper Kraft. The Stickies deal is off. But sales are up again. However, cash-flow crisis! House, mountain lot, nearly everything else owned are used as collateral to obtain a business loan.

March. Rickie Tickie Stickies are *the thing*. Don babbles for several minutes on Walter Cronkite's CBS evening newscast, more time than was given that evening to the Vietnam War! Euphoria!

Sales, sales. Work, work....

–1969–

180 million Rickie Tickies have been sold worldwide for more than $20 million retail. They are in Sweden, Argentina, Japan, Mexico, Germany, and Canada. Someone reports seeing Rickie Tickies on a taxi cab in Cairo. One is spotted in a phone booth in Tel Aviv. They turn up on Snoopy's doghouse in the *Charlie Brown* comic strip....

Problem: many of the flowers are "knock-offs"! The product pirates have moved in. Some interesting names: "Stick 'em ups," "Tackies..." Funny now, not then. The pirate wars begin, along with expansion, more cash flow crises. Work,

work, work...., and, finally, Rickie Tickie Stickies are solidly in the black. The fad dies.

New ventures begin....

–TODAY–

Twelve hundred, and counting, new products by Kracke are on the shelf, having sold for over a billion dollars retail.

"Overnight" success–every step of the way.

"Genius [*really*] is one percent inspiration and ninety-nine percent perspiration."

–Thomas Alva Edison

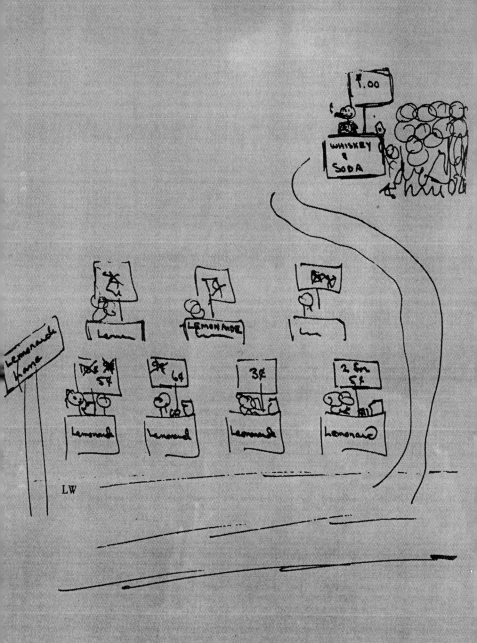

"Go where it ain't crowded."

-*Garrison Keillor*

Pick the right place and time

Garrison Keillor, at the height of his phenomenal success with *A Prairie Home Companion* on public radio, was asked what prompted him to choose radio as the showcase for his talents? Why hadn't he chosen one of the more popular mediums? He responded that as a young man he had been given some good advice and had simply followed it. "Go where it ain't crowded," a wise man had told him—

Keillor found in public radio a *niche* and planted himself within it, grew and flourished, and then moved on to explore possibilities in gardens larger and more lucrative.... Niches are wonderful little places to plant and nurture a talent or idea. They're "not crowded" which reduces the competitive pressures and increases the chances of getting a start. To grow and flourish you must first survive: that's trick number one, no matter the trade.

It's show time!

-an everyday saying

Performance after performance

Dr. Deming, the irascible old father of the modern Quality movement throughout the world–the original guru who went to Japan after World War II (we Americans wouldn't listen to him) and helped the Japanese get back on their feet and on their way to becoming world leaders in quality– was not, in contrast to most of the current Excellence, Quality ... gurus, merely a cheerleader. He did more than talk quality. In the context of business purpose and market forces, Dr. Deming taught a method of defining and achieving quality in the work place. His approach was practical, not philosophical.

The Deming approach:
define the work process,
understand the work process,
measure outcomes, and
communicate results.

Deming preached specificity and objectivity. He wanted results on the wall, quite literally, where *everyone* can see them. It boils down to this: clearly stated, realistic performance standards and direct performance feedback. *Information*, letting us know if we're winning or losing.

Winners love to be measured, losers hate it–all of us

91

need it! The Deming approach, as opposed to all the cheer leading that has come after, creates a realistic challenge to perform at high levels, not false expectations based on empty words. And it matters not whether you're a ballet dancer or ditch digger, or studying at the Sorbonne.

Discover (or rediscover) the hard-nosed common sense of Deming. Manage yourself (and others) through performance standards–objective, rational, clearly communicated *performance standards*–not good intentions or abstract notions of excellence.

It's performance that counts, performance after performance....

"[It's true!] Every man's work, whether it be literature or music or pictures or architecture or anything else, is always a portrait of himself."

–Samuel Butler

"No good decision was ever made in a swivel chair."

-General George S. Patton, Jr.

Stand-up decisions

Porter B. Williamson, who served with General Patton during World War II and has summarized the general's philosophy of management in his excellent book *Patton's Principles*, quotes the general: "I mean it! No good decision was ever made in a swivel chair! Better to have a decision made on horseback than in a swivel chair. A man in a swivel chair does not have his juices going right.... Get out of that swivel chair and know what's going on!"

Amen.

A decision maker who sits in one place is a sitting duck: ninety percent of the information he gets will be carefully arranged to confirm what he already believes (to make him happy) or to confirm what someone else believes and wants him to endorse (to make them happy) and that's not the stuff of good decisions. *Raw* data, not *cooked*, is needed to make good decisions, and for that you've got to get out and talk to the troops.

Surprise people; appear most anywhere, anytime. Be easy to talk to, keep your eyes and ears open. Keep the juices flowing. Sit in a swivel chair, if you must, to read or talk on the phone, but otherwise be on the move. Good decisions are made with good information by people in motion.

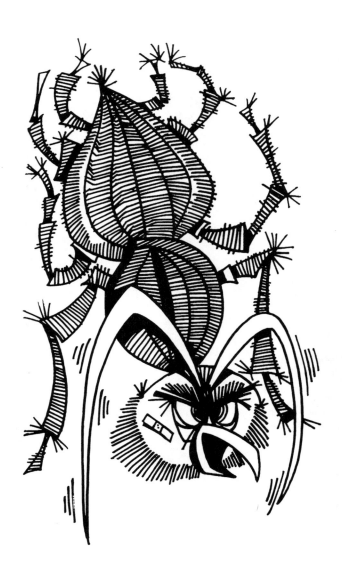

"If you've seen one cockroach, you haven't seen them all."

-the Orkin man

Do what you say you'll do, follow through

Stop and think—

If everyone who ever said to you "Let's have lunch" followed through, you'd probably be booked for the next hundred years. The *let's have lunch* routine is a social form, a gesture, we understand. Harmless enough (though we prefer a handshake and an honest "good-bye") if it stopped there. Unfortunately, it is often part of a larger pattern.

For instance, in our experience the let's-have-lunch sort of guy or gal in response to interest in a report or article that comes up in discussion often says, "Oh I'll send you that."

Gee, that's a generous offer, you think. "Gosh, thanks a lot."

But if the promised item never comes? Harmless again? We don't think so. It leaves a bad taste when there's no follow through. It crosses the line. It's bad business, a harbinger to the wary eye. If you've seen one cockroach–even if it's a little one–that's one too many. Look out, there's more. If you can't count on a person in little things–this may seem harsh, but we find it to be true–you can't count on him, period.

Happily, there's another side to this story—

Think about what happens when people do what they say they'll do, when men and women mean what they say.

What happens if someone tells you he wants to have lunch, or that he's going to send you something, and he does it? First of all, you're probably surprised, maybe even shocked. Unfortunately, it's not everyday that an indefinite invitation is followed up or when you receive an item that was casually promised. You're grateful, *impressed*. The person who follows through stands out among the many who say but don't do. Relationships and deals have a way of going forward, if not right away, later on. It's good business to mean what you say, as well as the right thing to do!

Make the commitment to following through. Work at it. Start with the little things like lunch invitations and keep right on through work schedules and performance commitments. Never fall into the trap of thinking you can successfully pick and choose when to do what you say you'll do: that's a slippery slope and you'll end up, sooner or later, sliding down. Do what you say you'll do! Don't say it if you don't mean it.

Of course, none of us bats a thousand at this, and none of us ever will. Every one of us slips from time to time and has to get back up with new resolve. Perfection should not be pretended. But if we, every one of us, work at it, we can do better–and we'll be better and stronger for the exercise.

Do we sound like your mother?

Well, she was right.

"IF YOU CAN'T GIVE ME YOUR WORD OF HONOR, WILL YOU GIVE ME YOUR PROMISE?"

–Samuel Goldwyn

Exit on time

Nothing lasts forever–remember the dinosaurs. The ability to adjust to change, to adapt, is an important trick, one that must be taken no matter the game. Sooner or later, it's adapt or die. Evolution, adaptation, survival of the fittest, whether you're a dinosaur or a businessman–or both–is a game you must play today so you can play tomorrow; the losers become fossils—

Move on, forge ahead, learn, grow, change. It's do something different–at least differently–or get buried, one way, one time or another, by some one or some thing.

There comes a time when nearly everything, products, processes, designs; offenses, defenses; strategies, styles ..., outlive their usefulness. They die.

Don't be there when it happens.

Vision

Jim Bridger, legend of the American western frontier, was a leader. Settlers followed him west, to settle new lands and make new homes and fulfill a nation's destiny. Jim Bridger had a vision of a place where a man and woman could build a future large and free.

Jim Bridger was a master storyteller. He painted pictures with his words. People listened to him and glimpsed a land across the prairie, over great mountains, beside the sea: a land not of milk and honey, one of hardship and danger; but where men and women were limited by only their own initiative and endurance, owned by no one, all under a sky so large that anything could be. Folks lined up to follow Jim west to a hard land of dreams.

Jim Bridger knew where he was going and why, and he could tell the story—his reputation for frontier eloquence endures, along with his deeds, as an essential dimension of any portrait of this mountain man. More than an adventurer, more than an explorer: he was a salesman and a pioneer. Bridger established settlements and taught people how to survive and kept them supplied, and kept them coming. He *led* people west, he didn't just show them the way.

Jim Bridger had a vision, purpose and pictures painted with words backed by the faith to act. That's why folks followed him west. *Purpose and pictures backed by the faith to act* in ventures as large as the settling of the American west or in our everyday work-lives, however mundane the day to day projects–*vision,* in ventures large or small–that's why any person willingly follows another, anytime, anywhere.

"Back of the beating hammer
  By which the steel is wrought
Back of the workshop's clamor
  The seeker may find the thought....
Back of the job–the dreamer
  Who's making the dream come true!"

–Berton Braley
The Thinker

"Integrity is the first step to true greatness."

-Charles Simmons

The foundation of leadership

Imagine a pyramid—
The cap is a leader's vision, what's over the mountain that others should follow him (or her) to discover or achieve. The middle block, supporting the cap, is a leader's ability to communicate this vision, to infect others with enthusiasm. The base of the pyramid, *the first step*, supporting all else, is integrity.

Leaders gain followers because of their vision and ability to communicate. They keep them because they have integrity, because they are steadfast and fair. Followers must believe that a leader will balance a personal concern for each man and woman he leads with the larger purpose for which he stands, and they must believe that he has grit, that he will stay the course, not abandon his troops in the face of adversity.

Vision raises the army and readies it for battle. But it is personal faith in the leader that keeps the troops marching through darkness when victory appears unattainable. People will lean in times of trouble not on a leader's vision but on the leader himself.

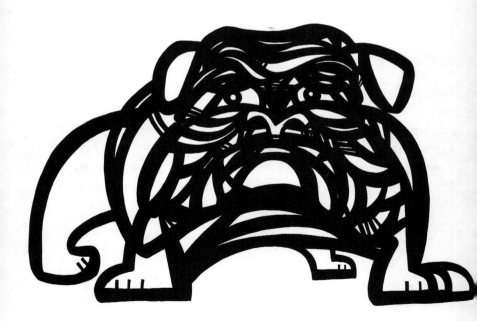

-*Lee Whipple*
from a graduation address

Integrity

Integrity is a thing *felt*, not seen. No oath of loyalty, no commendation, no single act, however true and bold, can hold it long enough before the eye for the mind to paint an adequate picture. No, to all these things, and more, that represent but can never be integrity—

Integrity is a bulldog stance, maintained, in peaceful times and those of trouble, that serves not self but larger, better, deeper things. Everybody *feels* its presence, everybody knows when it's there.

"We're all ignorant, just about different things."

Twenty-twenty listening

First man: "I've got a new hearing aid, it's fantastic."
Second man: "That's really tiny!"
First man: "Quarter to four."

Most of us, like the guy with new hearing aid, are totally confident of our ability to hear what the other guy says, totally sure of our ability to listen. That's the problem: *blindness*. For most of us it's not being deaf but a form of blindness that causes poor listening; and all the misunderstanding and missed opportunities that goes with it. *Observe* just how poorly you (even if you're among the best) listen and out of terror, anticipating all the mishaps and misses, you'll pay closer attention when another human being speaks.

"*Look*," as Shakespeare said, "with thine ears." Immediately you will learn a lot of new interesting-and-valuable things, and make a bunch of new friends. Listening is the cure for ignorance and more than half of good human relations.

When the donkey becomes too pleased with himself,
he goes down upon the ice to dance.
                                —an old German Proverb

Fear of personal loss is the forgotten motivator of our time.

-the authors

Motivating others

Consider Cortez in his attack from the sea against the Aztecs—
His men, attempting to take the beach, had been repulsed.
They were rowing back to the ships, beaten, in full retreat....
Cortez torched the ships, set them ablaze, burned them right
down to the water. His men turned around and took the
beach. Sometimes you have to give people very clear alter-
natives before they discover their true capabilities.

Cortez was in his way one heck of a leader. The son-of-a-
gun understood motivation, one aspect of it anyway. He
assessed correctly that his men were not fighting up to their
potential, and he lit a fire. It was do or die, and now! There
comes a time in almost every leader's life when it's now or
never, take the beach or get driven into the sea: a time to
burn the boats.

We know this is contrary to what the better schools teach.
They suggest motivating people through the better side
of human nature, tapping positive group dynamics and
individual aspirations. OK. We agree! It's at the heart of
much of what we've been saying all along. But it's not the
whole story. The lesson taught by Cortez is also true.
There are times and places—and certain people—that re-
quire the direct approach. Sometimes you have to burn

the boats right down to the water.

If you're going to be a responsible leader, responsible for results as well as your people, you'd best consider the whole enchilada when thinking about human behavior. The popular, half-baked theories of motivation that consider only the happier side of human nature are lovely to contemplate, but they aren't the whole story.

Balance, one more time.

"The *final test* [italics ours] of a leader is that he leaves behind him in other men the conviction and the will to carry on."

–Walter Lippmann

> *"There is something that is much more scarce, something finer far...than ability. It is the ability to recognize ability."*

-*Elbert Hubbard*

The fruit salad theory of managing others

The following was confided to us by the CEO of a Fortune 100 company–strictly off the record. He would never repeat it in public. Everyone would be shocked and dismayed, at least officially. Ironically, free expression of things not in keeping (however accurate and true) with the popular myths are becoming more and more forbidden fruit for those in power. So we especially appreciate our friend's candor, and we happen to think he's right!

"We've got a fruit salad of people around here," he told us. "We've got smart apples, second bananas, a few coconuts, and a sour grape or two. If we had all smart apples we wouldn't need any systems, procedures, policies, or rules. The smart apples know what to do, or can figure it out, and they'll do it, mostly. But we *don't* have just smart apples: we've got those second bananas and coconuts and those sour grapes too. And every once in a while, let's admit it, a bad apple in the mix.

"So we have to put the smart apples to work," he continued, "building systems, creating procedures and policies, making rules–so the second bananas and the coconuts will know what to do, and to keep the sour grapes and that occasional bad apple in line. Everyone would like to have a team of only smart apples–a little utopia of intelligence and willing cooperation–and it's unpopular to admit it's not like that. So everyone claims, officially, me included, that's it's all perfect teamwork, every one just as smart and just as good as everyone else, all sweetness and light. But it's not really like that. It's *fruit salad*, I'll tell you–it's the best you can do in this world–and you'd better get your smart apples on top."

That's the recipe.

No, the company was not Fruit of the Loom, not Del Monte....

"The genius of a good leader is to leave behind him a situation which common sense, without the grace of genius, can deal with successfully."

–Walter Lippmann

If all of us agree all of the time,
some of us don't need to be here.

-anonymous

Unanimous decisions

A unanimous decision, except in boxing or ice skating, means one of three things—

1) The decision was made in a back room somewhere and the vote was only a formality. In other words, the fix was in.

2) There was no decision to be made in the first place, a *no-brainer,* and the vote was only theatrical. Theater of the absurd, for our money.

3) There was no backbone in the decision making group and the vote was merely political, conforming to and confirming a "pecking order." *Who's who* not *what's what,* reflected.

Unanimity makes harmony, *not* good decisions. Harmony may be a trouble sign!
Disagreement is the stuff of which good decisions are born. Disagreement is the stuff of critical thinking. The open competition of one idea or course of action against another allows the stronger to emerge. Good decisions are the result of the back-and-forth and give-and-take of intelligent,

independent minds. There is no substitute.

Alfred P. Sloan, the genius who created the decision-making structure of the original General Motors organization, once dismissed a board meeting when he got a unanimous vote. All yeses. He sent the board away for two hours, instructing them to come back with some argument in *opposition*. He wanted some give-and-take before a decision was made. Sloan well understood that when everyone is thinking alike, chances are no one is thinking.

"I'm sorry sir, I don't understand.
What was it you wanted me to think?"

—Junior executives we've known
(and would as soon forget)

*"One who sets the entire army in motion
to chase an advantage will not attain it"*

-*Sun Tzu*
from The Art of War

Restraint

Total deployment is a shortcut to failure—no room to maneuver, no flexibility.

Surprises! Good leaders expect them, and they allocate resources in advance to deal with them. Sun Tzu summed it up eloquently in the first century B.C. General George S. Patton Jr. put it his way approximately two thousand years later: "If we cannot change battle plans, it's the same thing as digging a foxhole where the enemy will find us and put us in our graves.... Always keep something in reserve."

Sun Tzu to General Patton, yesterday and today, in business, school, sports..., as well as war, the advice is essential. Survival 101: *never* commit all your resources. Time, equipment, space, manpower, and money—hold a portion of these in reserve to deal with the unexpected, or the unexpected will sooner or later deal with you.

"To me, all of life is just a sketch..." -Don Kracke, July 1993

Never lose sight of your goals, or pursue them too closely.

-*the authors*

Rigidflexibility

Success is seldom a straight line—

The route to success is infrequently that of a locomotive pulling boxcars down the line. Success does not run on prelaid tracks. Success, worthy of the name, is always creating, never retracing a route. It cannot be measured in miles per hour, or kept to a schedule with stations laid out neatly along the way.

The route to success resembles, more than any modern rolling stock, that of the old frontier wagon train, weaving here and there around obstacles, changing course temporarily, suffering setbacks; yet moving, always, as the seasons pass, relentlessly on in the chosen direction, always, one way or another, heading west. Success is always and forever an adventure. Always creation.

The successful people we have known, almost to the woman and man, arrived at their present preeminence by the scenic route, zigzagging, switching horses, finding themselves, from time to time, on side roads and cul-de-sacs; but always finding a way back to the dream, the chosen direction, out of which their journey was born. Most of these folks, the ones who have shared with us the wisdom that we have shared with you, looking back, value the detours as much as any fast lane they have traveled. They have come to realize that no one ever really arrives and, if he has any sense, doesn't want to.

INDEX